American Symbols:

A Pictorial History

over 1100 illustrations

AMERICAN SYMBOLS

a pictorial history — compiled by ERNST LEHNER

introduction by ROGER BUTTERFIELD

WILLIAM PENN PUBLISHING CORP.,
NEW YORK

Grateful acknowledgment is hereby expressed to all the companies and organizations who granted permission to have their trademarks and insignia reproduced in this book.

LIBRARY OF CONGRESS CARD CATALOG NUMBER: 57-14579

MANUFACTURED IN THE UNITED STATES OF AMERICA
BY GANIS AND HARRIS, NEW YORK

CONTENTS

INTRODUCTION

THE RECORDED HISTORY of the New World began one day in 1492 when Christopher Columbus went ashore on Watling Island in the Caribbean and raised a flag with a green cross and the initials "F" and "Y". To the Spaniards who were with him the emblem had a clear and compelling meaning —henceforth the island was to be ruled by their most Christian majesties, Ferdinand and Ysabel. The natives who stood by and watched of course had no idea of what was going on. But they soon learned of the powerful significance that could be contained in a few symbols.

Today, in an age of pictures and television, the nation's symbols are more meaningful to us and to the rest of the world than ever. Some of them such as Uncle Sam and the American eagle, are so familiar that we have come to take them for granted. Others which served their purpose for a time have long since been forgotten, and it is a valuable thing to see them again as one can in this book. Among the many competing symbols that were used to represent the early nation or its various sections were a buxom Indian maiden wearing a tobacco-leaf apron (she ended-up on the flag and seal of Florida), a bucking horse, a beaver, codfish, deer, a red French liberty cap (buried now in the seals of the Senate and War Office), and a pine or palmetto tree.

The Esteemed Rattlesnake

Probably none of these were as widely used at the time of the Revolution on American battle flags and drums as the rattlesnake, which appeared often with a printed warning: "DON'T TREAD ON ME!" (See Page 56.) As early as 1754 the rattlesnake was used by Franklin in a political cartoon intended to unite the thirteen colonies; the snake appeared cut into sections, labeled with sectional names (the head represented the New England colonies), and given the caption: "JOIN OR DIE."

A writer in a newspaper at the time of the Revolution explained the significance of this fighting symbol as follows:

"The rattlesnake is found in no other quarter of the globe than America . . . Her eye exceeds in brightness that of any other animal, and she has no eyelids. She may therefore be esteemed an emblem of vigilance. She never begins an attack, nor, when once engaged, ever surrenders. She is therefore an emblem of magnanimity and true courage . . . She never wounds until she has generously given notice, even to her enemy . . . One of her rattles, singly, is incapable of producing sound; but the ringing of thirteen together is sufficient to alarm the boldest man living . . ."

British cartoonists were quick to accept the rattlesnake as the embodiment of the American Revolution, and they made use of the symbol according to their political sentiments. One unfriendly artist drew an American snake presenting a French soldier with a basketful of squirming frogs. "Monsieur, be pleased to accept these frogs; I have just killed them in the bogs," says the snake, to which the Frenchman replies: "I give you thanks, my good Ally; Some will make Soup, the rest a Fry!" (But the libel did little harm as evidenced by the gift, from the French people to America a century later, which has become one of our most widely known symbols: The Statue of Liberty.)

Another London cartoonist, more sympathetic to the Yankee cause, pictured a mighty rattlesnake coiled around Cornwallis' army at Yorktown, with the following words coming from its mouth:

"Two British armies I have thus Burgoyn'd
And room for more I've got behind!"

Still another British sympathizer, Edmund Burke, the great parliamentary orator, used the color symbols of Washington's army—"the buff and the gray"—as his own sartorial motif when he went to the House of Commons, and he tried to get all of his friends to do so, too.

It could not be expected that the creeping rattlesnake would win general acceptance as a symbol for the high-flying young United States. The desire for a proper symbol was strong in the minds of the men who wrote and adopted the Declaration of Independence. On July 4, 1776, the very day that independence was finally approved, the Continental Congress appointed a committee to design a national seal. The members were Benjamin Franklin, John Adams, and Thomas Jefferson. Their deliberations dragged on for years, and eventually were completed by other men. The result firmly established the American eagle as the national bird and official symbol.

Franklin, who had gone to France before the final action, was disappointed; he thought the wild turkey should have been chosen instead. He complained in a letter to his daughter that the eagle made its living by stealing fish from other birds, and "Besides, he is a rank coward; the little *king-bird,* not bigger than a sparrow, attacks him boldly and drives him out of the district." But perhaps Franklin was not being too serious. The eagle has long been regarded as the symbol of dignity and power, and was so used by great nations from very ancient times. Indeed, the eagle rode on top of the Roman legions' standards, and the patriotic talk of the time—after a Roman army had been defeated by the barbarians—was "to get the eagles back." And Caesar once, the story goes, turned his tenth legion into the legend it has become, by taking away its eagle after the legion had hesitated in battle.

Deep, Mighty, and Keen

A recent writer has given the American eagle full credit in these appropriate terms: "He is deep in the chest, mighty in wingspread, and keen of eye. In brief, he has the qualities which have carried our nation through all its crises, and which are now invoked once more."

During the Revolution, and for many years afterward, little attention was paid to another famous symbol of American freedom—the Liberty Bell in Philadelphia. It is true enough that the Bell did not ring on the first Fourth of July, in 1776, because the Congress was still in secret session that day. But it did help to make the first announcement of independence a few days later, and it played a leading part in all patriotic occasions up to the time it suffered a fatal crack while tolling the knell of Chief Justice John Marshall, in 1835. After that the City Councils of Philadelphia ordered a new bell cast, and tried to throw in the broken Liberty Bell as scrap metal in part payment for the new one!

Luckily the bell-maker decided that the cost of hauling the bell to his shop was more than its metal was worth, and he refused to take it away. So for a decade or so the silent Bell stood in a corner of the old State House, where visitors could read the words that were stamped around its top: PROCLAIM LIBERTY THROUGHOUT THE LAND UNTO ALL THE INHABITANTS THEREOF. Gradually it dawned on some people that this message was the most prophetic coincidence in all of American history; for the Bell was originally made in 1752, more than twenty years before the Revolution. The Pennsylvania legislators who ordered it from England had selected their text from the Bible (Leviticus 25:10) and they chose the very one that most completely expressed the Bell's historic and legendary role. Romantic writers began broadcasting the Bell's story, with embellishments from their own imaginations. By 1876, when the nation celebrated its centennial, the Bell had become a treasured relic and symbol.

Strangely enough, there is no way to trace the authentic history of the most important symbol of all—the American Flag itself. Congress did not get around to designing the new flag until almost a year after independence was declared, and then only a short resolution was passed and entered on the record: "*Resolved,* that the flag of the thirteen United States be thirteen stripes alternate red and white; that the union shall be thirteen stars, white in a blue field, representing a new constellation." There is no account of debates or discussions to tell us how these symbols were chosen, or who chose them. There is reason to believe that flags of this description, or much like it, were already in use, and that Congress was acting simply to make the existing flag official.

Betsy Ross, of course, had been busy making flags for the Pennsylvania Navy, for she was a professional seamstress who would naturally be called on for such patriotic and useful work. But the story of how she designed the "first flag" for George Washington is only a story, supported by family hearsay. The origin and evolution of the flag is extremely complicated and obscure, and lacking in any convincing documentation up to the year 1818.

At that time, due to the lobbying activities of a

Navy captain named Samuel C. Reid, Congress finally passed a specific law which standardized the United States flag at thirteen red and white stripes, with one white star for every state on a field of blue. Even as late as the War of 1812 our Navy vessels were flying "American" flags of red, white and blue stripes, varied numbers of stars and stripes, and yellow flags with eagles and rattlesnake embelms.

Every nation evolves its best symbols as it goes along, and this is especially true of our own Uncle Sam. The lanky rube with the swallow-tail coat and flag-striped trousers was created by a brilliant group of cartoonists who flourished after the Civil War. They borrowed his rural innocence from the original Yankee Doodle, and his costumes—including the tall beaver hat—from Brother Jonathan, a favorite cartoon character in the age of Andrew Jackson. They gave him the same initials as the nation, and in 1869 they added the sprouting chin whiskers that have been his indispensable trademark ever since. In the final form that we know today, Uncle Sam is a remarkable mixture of simplicity and guile, of fatherly affection and stern fighting spirit—a kindly old-fashioned gentleman when things are right, but a hard-fisted terror to evildoers when aroused by something wrong.

Our Own Political Zoo

Unlike the official emblems on the flag and the national seal, Uncle Sam is uniquely American; his origin cannot be traced beyond our border lines. The same can be said of many of the pictorial images to be found in the pages that follow. For Americans have always had a knack for creating their own symbols, and for making them serve many purposes.

Examples abound in this book of this creative knack. The minuteman of Concord was used as symbol in the last war. The Fife and Drum trio of 1776 is recognized throughout the world as the symbol of a victorious, hard-fighting yet cheerful American spirit. The buffalo, the covered wagon, Mississippi paddle wheel steamers, Paul Bunyan with his blue ox, and other folk myths—such as the yarns about our Western badmen and their

tendency to become Robin Hoods on TV—all point to a country that has invented, adapted and used symbols with exuberant abandon. Among other things we have created our own political zoo—the Republican elephant, the Democratic donkey, the Tammany tiger, and most marvelous of all, the grinning, insatiable mythological beast known as the Gerrymander. Hats—ranging from Davy Crockett's coonskin to Al Smith's brown derby—have become well-understood symbols. The Indians have supplied us with any number of symbols, from the head on the five-cent piece to the peace pipe on Oklahoma's state seal.

We have also assimilated many symbols from older nations and cultures. The Amish "hex" signs which can be seen on barns from the Pennsylvania Turnpike are derived from old German religious motifs of flowers and sacred objects. The cattle brands of our open range were invented by the Spaniards who brought the first cattle to the new world, by way of Mexico. And the country which fought hard to disentangle itself from European aristocracy has made free use of the aristocrats' favorite symbol—the heraldic shield, which appears in many of our family, business and official emblems.

This book is a fascinating collection of the signs and symbols that influenced American history and American life. So far as I know this is the first attempt to bring together the more famous symbols, not only of patriotism and great events, but also from the fields of business and advertising, political campaigns and parties, railroads, automobiles and aviation, colleges, baseball, folklore, and even comic strips. There is a complete guide to the seals and other official emblems of all the fifty states.

Altogether there is a wealth of unusual information here for every American who wants to know more about his country. The book will also be a delight to the artist, and a unique work of reference for the student and scholar. Essentially a symbol is a short-cut to convey information at a glance, and that is why the practical-minded Americans have found them so useful across the last 350 years.

ROGER BUTTERFIELD

This New World

COLON.

CHRISTOPHER COLUMBUS' COAT
OF ARMS WHEN HE WAS MADE
DUKE OF VERAGUA

VINLAND OR INDIA?

WHEN THE ITALIAN seaman, Christopher Columbus, sailed to Iceland in 1477, he undoubtedly heard how Leif Erickson had been blown off his course almost 500 years before and landed in the Nova Scotia-New England area. To Columbus this may have meant that the new land was not Vinland, but the world described by Marco Polo as the richest place on earth—the Orient.

By 1492 Columbus had convinced Ferdinand and Isabella of Spain that he could sail west to India. On August 3rd he started out and on October 12th he saw land. After exploring the Bahamas and sailing along the north coast of Cuba and Haiti, he returned to Spain a hero. Yet after three more trips—and de Gama's actual passage to India around the African cape in 1497—he died a broken lonely man in 1506, still insisting he had found the Orient.

The next year a German geographer, Waldseemuller, suggested the new world be named after Amerigo Vespucci, an Italian navigator who had sailed to what is now South America.

THE MAN FOR WHOM AMERICA WAS NAMED—*AMERIGO VESPUCCI*,
FROM THE NEW MAP DRAWN BY WALDSEEMULLER IN 1507

COLUMBUS SAILED on his first trip to America with three ships: the *Nina,* the *Pinta,* and the *Santa Maria.* His voyage, beset by near mutinies and fear of the unknown, was not followed immediately by a stream of eager settlers. A little over one hundred years later the settlers began to arrive after the new world began to look better than the old, and after such inducements as below broadcasting the fact that there were "Excellent fruites by planting in Virginia." It was not India but, as prophesied, it was rich.

FIRST PRINTED PICTURE OF COLUMBUS' LARGEST SHIP, THE SANTA MARIA, FROM HIS REPORT IN 1494

WOODCUT OF VIRGINIA COMPANY TRADER FROM FIRST "TRAVEL POSTER" ADVERTISING TRIPS TO THE NEW VIRGINIA COLONY. LONDON—1612

DUTCH WEST INDIA COMPANY FLEET ILLUSTRATION FROM FIRST CHARTER FOR THE SETTLERS OF NEW NETHERLAND, NOW NEW YORK. AMSTERDAM—1630

**FIRST CHART OF AMERICA AS A SEPARATE
CONTINENT, BY MUNSTER, BASEL—1542**

**THE MICHAEL LOK MAP SHOWING NORTH AMERICA
FROM FLORIDA TO CANADA—1582**

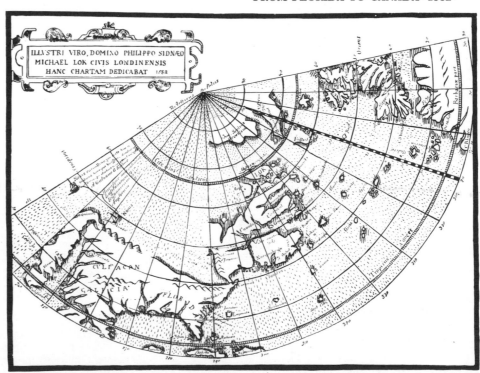

WITH THE DUTCH in New York, the British in New England and Virginia (which at the time extended to the Mississippi), the Spanish in Florida, and the French in Canada and throughout the Great Lakes region, the large European powers set the stage for the inevitable fight to gain control of the new world with its fertile land, wild game, furs, timber, and taxes. For now the settlers came, hacked out a living, fought Indians and survived.

THE KINGS COUNCIL, COLONY OF VIRGINIA—1606

NEW PLYMOUTH COLONY—1620

NEW NETHERLANDS—1623

MASSACHUSETTS COLONY—1628

PETER STUYVESANT
GOVERNOR OF NEW AMSTERDAM—1642

VIRGINIA COLONY AFTER RESTORATION—1652

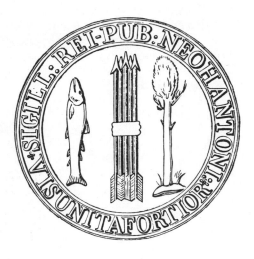

NEW HAMPSHIRE COLONY—1680

WILLIAM PENN, GOVERNOR AND PROPRIETOR
OF PENNSYLVANIA—1682

THE OHIO COMPANY—1749

JOHN MURRAY, EARL OF DUNMORE
GOVERNOR OF VIRGINIA—1772

SURVIVAL was difficult. The Virginia Company of London, chartered in 1606, established a colony at Jamestown only to abandon it a few years later because of the losing struggle against the wilderness—even though Captain John Smith worked and fought to keep it going. The Ohio Company, formed under a grant from George II and made up of Virginians, would have prospered except for the French and Indian War in 1756, which caused the defenceless settlers to flee.

ON DECEMBER 21st, 1620, the 180 ton *Mayflower* touched the coast at Plymouth with 108 Pilgrims from England. They formed the Mayflower Compact, the first example of a written constitution in North America, and functioned for 70 years without a charter from the King. In 1691 they united with the Massachusetts Bay Colony. (The Rock was moved inland.) One of the most outstanding Colonial leaders was an English lawyer who became a Quaker and, in payment of a debt to his father by the King, was granted Pennsylvania—William Penn. He made peace with the Indians, and set up the first public school.

THE MAYFLOWER

PLYMOUTH ROCK—
NEW WORLD STEPPING-STONE

By the Royts, from "My Country," Webster Pub. Co.

PEACE-MAKER WILLIAM PENN,
WITH INDIAN FRIEND

WILLIAMSBURG WAS the temporary capital of Virginia from 1676 to 1699 and was made capital from 1699 to 1799. The College of William and Mary was established in 1693 and the Raleigh Tavern was to be the meeting place of Jefferson, Henry, and other revolutionaries who wrote the first drafts of the Declaration of Independence there. Restoration of the city was begun in 1927 and it is now as it was in 1700.

RESTORED GOVERNOR'S PALACE IN WILLIAMSBURG, VIRGINIA

The Young Country

FIGHT FOR INDEPENDENCE

ON DECEMBER 16th, 1773, a group of angry Bostonians dumped $90,000 worth of tea into their harbor to protest the tariffs and heavy taxes imposed by the British. Harsh laws resulted, and so did the first Continental Congress. To stamp out the threatening uproar, British General Gage marched on Concord in April, 1775, to seize the arsenal and arrest two trouble-makers: Hancock and Samuel Adams. But the Minutemen of Lexington and Concord, alerted by Revere's ride, turned back the troops, destroyed one-fourth of them, and harassed the rest back to Boston. The Declaration of Independence was published the following year, and in 1777 Betsy Ross made the new flag. By 1783 the Colonies were free.

SPIRIT OF '76 (AFTER A. M. WILLARD)

FIRST OFFICIAL FLAG, 1777, MADE BY BETSY ROSS

PAUL REVERE'S RIDE APRIL 16, '75

INDEPENDENCE HALL, PHILA. HERE 2nd CONGRESS MET—1775

CONCORD MINUTEMAN

CARPENTER'S HALL, PHILADELPHIA, HERE 1st CONGRESS MET IN 1774 OVER TAXES

LIBERTY BELL, CAST IN 1753

PARTIALLY BURNED by the British in the War of 1812, the Capitol in Washington is 751 feet long and 350 feet wide. It contains 431 rooms, including the House and Senate, and the grounds cover 131 acres. It was designed and first put up in 1793, but changed many times since. The White House got its present name in 1902 through Congress because President Theodore Roosevelt asked for the change. The white paint was used after the War of 1812 when the charred house was repaired. Built in 1792, the White House was repaired once again between 1948 and 1952 since it was in danger of collapsing. The three-story West wing was added in 1902. There are now 132 rooms.

MOUNT VERNON, VIRGINIA, WASHINGTON'S HOME, BUILT 1743. USED BY HIM BEFORE THE WAR AND ON HIS RETIREMENT

FRANKLIN'S BIRTHPLACE, 1706-1790, BOSTON

CAPITOL—WASHINGTON, D.C. HOME OF THE U.S.A. CONGRESS

THE WHITE HOUSE—OFFICIAL HOME OF THE PRESIDENT

HOME OF JOHN & JOHN QUINCY ADAMS, BRAINTREE, MASS., NOW QUINCY

MONTICELLO, DESIGNED AND BUILT BY JEFFERSON ON HIS PLANTATION NEAR CHARLOTTESVILLE, VA.

THE FLAG of Commodore Perry's flagship, the *Lawrence*, had as its motto, "Don't Give Up the Ship!" During the battle of Lake Erie, in the War of 1812, the *Lawrence* began to sink, so Perry transferred the flag to the *Niagara* and continued to fight. The same spirit prevailed in the Alamo.

HOME OF PRESIDENT JAMES MADISON, 1751-1836, NEAR MONTPELLIER, VIRGINIA

JAMES MONROE'S HOME, MONTPELLIER. 1758-1831

THE U.S.S. "CONSTITUTION," KNOWN AS "OLD IRONSIDES" —WAR OF 1812

THE HERMITAGE—HOME OF ANDREW JACKSON, "OLD HICKORY," 1767-1845

THE ALAMO, WHERE 220 TEXANS DIED IN 1836 RESISTING 7,000 MEXICAN TROOPS FOR 12 DAYS

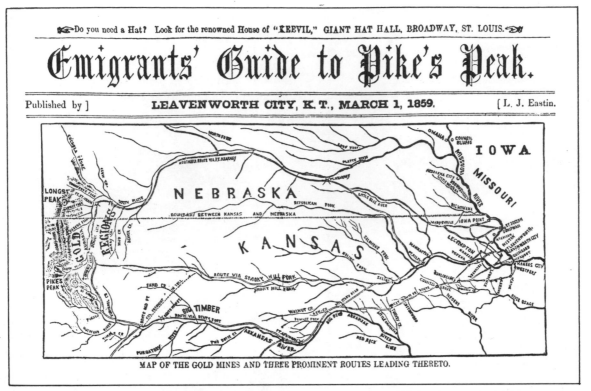

THE DISCOVERY OF GOLD IN WHAT IS NOW CALIFORNIA, COLORADO, NEVADA,
UTAH, AND ARIZONA IN THE 1840'S, STARTED A MASS MIGRATION WEST.
A WHOLE NEW INDUSTRY GOT THE MINERS THERE.

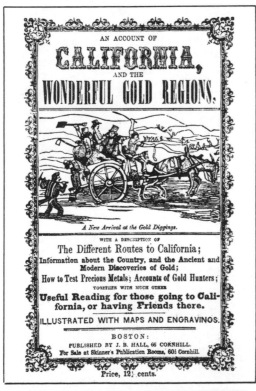

GUIDE TO THE GOLD FIELDS, PRINTED
IN BOSTON, 1849, HAD ALCHEMY TIPS

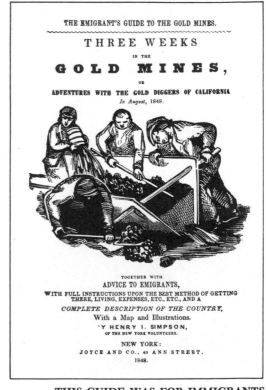

THIS GUIDE WAS FOR IMMIGRANTS
WHO WANTED TO GET RICH

THE BUFFALO

THE MOVE WEST was made on foot, by wagon, on horse, mule, scow, and steamboat. The first mule-drawn wagon train of ten wagons left St. Louis in 1830 and went over the Oregon trail. By 1849 more than 5,500 wagon trains were going to California and Oregon each year. They went through Indian raids (but back East the Indian was the peaceful tobacco tout in front of a store), storms, and buffalo stampedes—which sometimes also gave them food. The trains averaged 10 to 15 miles a day. In the early 1860's a pioneer could send a letter from Sacramento back to St. Louis for $5. The letter would go 1,980 miles by Pony Express with horse changes at 190 stations involving 80 riders and 420 horses, through the wild Indian land. At the same time luxurious steamboats plied commerce along the major, inhabited rivers.

PONY EXPRESS MONEY

WAGON TRAIN GOING WEST IN THE MIDDLE EIGHTIES TO NEW LAND

A MISSISSIPPI SIDE-WHEEL PACKET LOADING COTTON FOR NEW ORLEANS

THE CIGAR-STORE INDIAN

THE SECESSION of the Southern states, beginning in December, 1860, brought to a head the issues which had been smouldering for 40 years. At the outbreak of the war in 1861, the Union totaled 23 states with 22,000,000 people, while the Confederacy consisted of 11 states and 9,000,000 people, including 3,500,000 slaves. At the end of the war in April, 1865, the Confederacy had less than 175,000 men under arms. The Union army had about 800,000. During the cruel struggle the South lost more than 133,000 soldiers.

BIRTHPLACE OF ROBERT E. LEE
FREDRICKSBURG, VA. 1807-1870

THE BLUE & THE GRAY

CONFEDERATE SEAL

CONFEDERACY CAPITOL, RICHMOND

ABRAHAM LINCOLN, 1809-65; MONUMENT
DEDICATED IN 1922, WASHINGTON, D.C.

TOMB OF ULYSSES S. GRANT, 1822-1885,
UNION GENERAL, PRESIDENT, 1868-1876

WHILE THE WOUNDS of the Civil War slowly healed, the country consolidated its western land, purchased Alaska (1867), admitted more states, accepted the Statue of Liberty from France (1883), and became the earth's "melting pot." It also fought an 8-month war with Spain (1898) which not only freed Cuba, but announced to the world that the radical experiment in democracy was now a major world power to be reckoned with. In the new 20th-Century two world wars would prove that.

THE STAR SPANGLED BANNER
THE STARS AND STRIPES
OLD GLORY

REMEMBER
THE MAINE

"REMEMBER THE MAINE!" WAR-CRY
SPANISH-AMERICAN WAR, 1898

STATUE OF LIBERTY
N .Y. HARBOR, 1883

THE BALD EAGLE

GREAT SEAL OF
THE UNITED STATES OF AMERICA

"UNCLE SAM"

Made in America

FOLK AND MYTH CHARACTERS

AS THE GREAT country grew so did its legends, literature, and folk tales. Washington Irving (1783-1859) had already contributed *The Legend of Sleepy Hollow* and *Rip Van Winkle*. Mark Twain (or rather Samuel Clemens, 1835-1910) added Tom Sawyer and Huck Finn. Davey Crockett had written his own exciting biography before being killed in the Alamo. The gigantic Paul Bunyan ruled in the Northwest, while John Henry built the railroads and the West produced the clan of Billy the Kid, Jesse James, Doc Holiday, Wyatt Earp, Wild Bill Hickok, and Buffalo Bill. One representative for the women was Calamity Jane.

PAUL BUNYAN

HUCK FINN

RIP VAN WINKLE

DAVEY CROCKETT

TOM SAWYER

POSTER FROM BUFFALO BILL'S WILD WEST SHOW—
W. F. CODY (1846-1917)

AS THE COUNTRY developed its own culture, two forces impressed themselves upon the social and moral growth of its people. One was the frontier man. In the name of the one and only Buffalo Bill generations of young boys identified forever the buckskin with William Frederick Cody, who brought his wild west show to the eager East. At the same time the West provided the "good guy" and the "bad guy." The other force was the roles assumed by women as they fought for votes, dignity, and freedom. The girls who followed Mrs. Amelia Bloomer put on pants. The Gibson Girl enhanced the Gay '90's, and the Flapper the "roaring '20's."

AMERICAN COWBOY

WESTERN BAD-MAN

THE TOWN MARSHALL

THE BLOOMER GIRL, FOLLOWER
OF A. J. BLOOMER (1818-94)

THE GIBSON GIRL, CREATED
BY C. D. GIBSON (1867-1944)

THE FLAPPER, AFTER
JOHN HELD, JR.

WHEN WORD WENT throughout the Rhine valley near Switzerland in the early 1600's that William Penn would help the persecuted Mennonites move to America, many found their way to Pennsylvania, bringing their primitive designs with them.

THE MERMAID
(PROPHECY)

THE TREE OF LIFE
(FERTILITY)

AMISH BARN DESIGNS, POPULARLY CALLED "HEX SIGNS," ARE DRAWN AND PAINTED FOR DECORATIVE PURPOSES

SINCE 1683 THE MENNONITES, or Amish (or Pennsylvania Dutch, from the corruption of *Deutsch*), have added their own unique folkways to American and Canadian life. Their designs appear in embroidery, on wood and metal work, and crockery.

THE EPHRATA LILY
(THE PURE AND BEAUTIFUL)

THE DISTELFINK
(MOTHERLY LOVE)

MANY BARN DESIGNS ARE DERIVED FROM THE STARS,
MOON, SUN, AND OTHER SYMBOLS OF FERTILITY AND LIFE

SINCE ALL STEERS look much the same, and because there were no fences on the miles of grazing lands, brands soon became essential western symbols. The marks and designs are the heraldry of the plains.

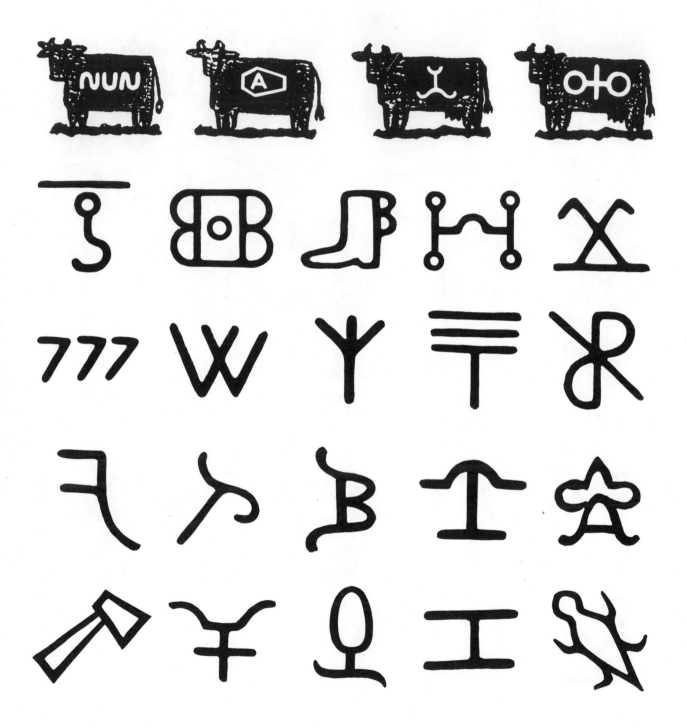

Top Row: Nunn Ranch, A. Coffin Ranch, Andiron, O-Cross-O; *Second Row:* Bar-Button-Hook, Bob-On-the-Square, Boot-B, Bridle-Bit, Buzzard-on-the-rail; *Third Row:* Chain-Seven, Crossed-W, Crow-Foot, Curry-Comb, Double-R; *Fourth Row:* Drag-F, Drunken-T, Flying-B, Hash Knife, Hat-A; *Bottom Row:* Hatchet, Longhorn-Plus, Laurel Leaf, Lazy-H, and Lizzard.

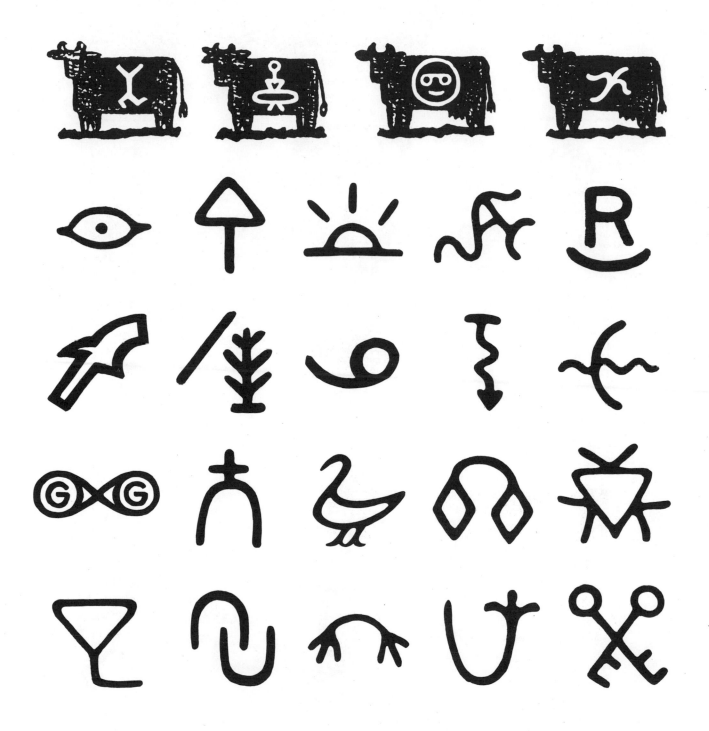

Top Row: Walking-Y, Old Woman Ranch, Owl Ranch, Wind Flower Ranch; ***Second Row:*** Pigs Eye, Pine Tree, Rising Sun, Running Sack, Rocking-R; ***Third Row:*** Six-Shooter, Slash-Pine, Sleeping Six, Snake-in-Moon; ***Fourth Row:*** Spectacle-G Spur, Swan, Swinging-Diamonds, Triangle-X; ***Bottom Row:*** Triangle-Tail, Tumbling Horseshoes, Turkey-Track, U-Fly, and Walking Tadpole.

Continent on the Move

TODAY OUR super-highways run over many of the old "Prairie Schooner" trails, from one coast to the other. Now, in one day, we can drive distances that would have taken pioneers more than a month's time.

COVERED CONASTOGA PRAIRIE FREIGHT WAGON
PHILADELPHIA TO PITTSBURGH IN 20 DAYS (1790)

SUNRISE TRAIL
NEW YORK—NEW JERSEY

SCENIC HIGHWAY
FLORIDA—MANITOBA, CANADA

BALTIMORE PIKE
PENNSYLVANIA—MARYLAND

BRIDGE ROUTE
NEW YORK—NEW JERSEY

CAPITOL TRAIL
PENNSYLVANIA—GEORGIA

WHITE HORSE TRAIL
NEW JERSEY

LEE HIGHWAY
NEW YORK—CALIFORNIA

LIBERTY HIGHWAY
NEW YORK—OHIO

LONE STAR ROUTE
ILLINOIS—TEXAS

WILLIAM PENN HIGHWAY
NEW YORK—PENNSYLVANIA

YELLOWSTONE TRAIL
MASSACHUSETTS—WASHINGTON

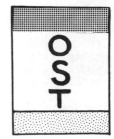

OLD SPANISH TRAIL
FLORIDA—CALIFORNIA

SUSQUEHANNA TRAIL
N. Y.–DISTRICT OF COLUMBIA

STAGECOACH ROUTE 1854
KALAMAZOO–GRAND RAPIDS

APPALACHIAN HIGHWAY
FLORIDA–QUEBEC

WOODPECKER ROUTE
SOUTH CAROLINA–FLORIDA

PONY EXPRESS TRAIL
MISSOURI–CALIFORNIA

TRADEMARK OF THE PACIFIC COAST BORAX COMPANY SINCE 1891
THE 20-MULE-TEAM TRAIN ROUTE, DEATH VALLEY–MOJAVE

INDIANA TOLL ROAD
156 MILES

KANSAS TURNPIKE
236 MILES

MAINE TURNPIKE
107 MILES

NEW JERSEY TURNPIKE
118 MILES

NEW YORK THRUWAY
427 MILES

OHIO TURNPIKE
214 MILES

PENNSYLVANIA TURNPIKE
360 MILES

WEST VIRGINIA
88 MILES

RAILROADS SOON became part of the landscape in America. At first, in the early 1800's, they were stage coaches on iron-covered wood rails pulled by horses. Then the early steam engines came into use. The first charter was given to the Mohawk & Hudson Company in 1825. Peter Cooper's Canton Iron Works built their first engine for them *(below left)* in 1829. That same year Cooper also built the first locomotive for the Baltimore and Ohio. It was called the Tom Thumb *(below right)*. This was the same Peter Cooper who financed the laying of the Atlantic cable, 1857-58, and built Cooper Union in New York. By 1880 the sprawling railroad industry laid more than 30,000 miles of track. Today there are more than 230,000 miles of track stretching from coast to coast, border to border, over the land.

MOHAWK & HUDSON'S 1st ENGINE 1829

BALTIMORE & OHIO'S TOM THUMB

GULF, MOBILE &
OHIO RAILROAD

"DE WITT CLINTON" BUILT IN 1831 FOR THE BALTIMORE & OHIO

LOUISVILLE &
NASHVILLE R.R.

NEWCASTLE & FRENCHTOWN R.R. LINE, 1833

"JUPITER" BUILT IN 1871 FOR THE CENTRAL PACIFIC R.R.

PENNSYLVANIA
RAILROAD

NEW HAVEN
RAILROAD

CHESAPEAKE &
OHIO RAILROAD

"CAMELBACK" BUILT BY ROSS WINANS FOR THE B. & O. 1873

ALTHOUGH STEAM-DRIVEN "AUTO" mobiles had been designed before the 1800's, it was not until Daimler of France built his gasoline-powered motor-cycle in 1885 and Benz of Germany his gasoline-driven auto in '86 that America produced true cars. In 1892, two brothers, Charles E. and Frank Duryea made a car, followed by Henry Ford, 1893, and Elwood Haynes in 1894. After the first War Ford mass-produced cars and the industry became gigantic in size.

Top illustration: Steam carriage by Dudgeon, New York, 1860; *Second Row:* The first automobile advertisement in the "Horseless Age," 1895; *Third Row:* Haynes, 1895-1925; Stanley Steamer, 1896-1926; Columbia, 1897-1925; *Fourth Row:* Autocar, since 1897; Backer Electric, 1899-1924; Jeffrey-Rambler, 1900-1913; *Bottom Row:* White-Stanhope Steamer, 1902-1912; Locomobile, 1899-1929; Lozier, 1902-1914.

Top Row: Peerless, 1900-1932; Thomas Flyer, 1902-1913; *Second Row:* Mitchell, 1902-1923; Pierce-Arrow, 1901-1938; Crestmobile, 1903-1905; *Third Row:* Stevens-Duryea, 1902-1926; Franklin, 1902-1934; Willys-Knight, 1903-1933; Nordyke-Marmon, 1903-1933; Auburn, 1903-1936; *Fourth Row:* Premier, 1903-1925; Maxwell, 1904-1925; Willys-Overland, 1903-1926; *Fifth Row:* Apperson, 1905-1926; American Austin, 1906-1919; Mercer, 1906-1925; Oakland-Pontiac, 1907-1931; Chalmers, 1908-1924; *Bottom Row:* Crawford, 1905-1924; Hupmobile, 1908-1941; Stoddard-Dayton, 1905-1913.

Top Row: Cole, 1909-1925; Scripps-Booth, 1911-1922; *Second Row:* McIntyre, 1908-1916; Saxon, 1911-1923; Lexington, 1913-1926; *Third Row:* Stutz, 1912-1936; Jordan, 1916-1932; Dupont, 1919-1929; Essex-Hudson, 1919-1933; Lafayette, 1920-1924; *Fourth Row:* Duesenberg, 1920-1927; Durant-Star, 1922-J928; Rickenbacker, 1922-1927; *Fifth Row:* Cord-Auburn, 1929-1937; Imperial-Chrysler, 1930; Dover-Hudson, 1930; Graham-Paige, 1930-1941; Royal-Reo, 1934; *Bottom Row:* La Salle-Cadillac, 1927-1940; Frazer-Kaiser, 1947; Americar-Willys, 1940.

Top Row: Founding dates follow name. Oldsmobile (General Motors) since 1897; Packard, 1899; Cadillac (General Motors), 1902; *Second Row:* Willys, since 1903; Ford, 1903; Studebaker (Nash) 1904; Buick (Chrysler), 1904; Hudson, 1909; *Third Row:* Pontiac (General Motors), since 1907; Dodge (Chrysler), 1914; Chevrolet (General Motors), 1911; *Fourth Row:* Nash (Studebaker), since 1917; Lincoln (Ford), 1917; Body by Fisher (General Motors), 1922; Chrysler, 1923; DeSoto (Chrysler), 1928; *Bottom Row:* Keystone Automobile Club, founded 1908; Mercury (Ford), 1938; Plymouth (Chrysler), 1929; Kaiser (Willys), 1947; American Automobile Association, 1910.

WRIGHT BROTHER'S BIPLANE, 1903

WHILE SAMUEL P. LANGLEY was experimenting with the first attempts to build airplanes that would do more than glide, Wilbur and Orville Wright worked in their bicycle shop in Dayton, Ohio. In 1903 the two brothers flew a plane that was "heavier than air" at Kitty Hawk, North Carolina. The first flight, with Orville at the controls, went 120 feet. It took him 12 seconds. Less than fifty years later, on the 8th of November, 1950, near Sinuiju, Korea, jet planes fought for the first time. Four U. N. jets hit 8 to 12 Communist planes, downing one. Jet airliners have made the world a shrunken globe.

NORTH AMERICAN   **SIKORSKY**   **NORTHROP**

BY THE MIDDLE of this century airlines were flying almost 5 billion passenger-miles in the United States in one year. In the last war more than 300,000 military planes were produced (through 1945). In one year—1944—96,318 war planes left the ground. Now we are in the age of rockets. During the International Geo-Physical Year, 1957-58, work progressed in the United States to send up rockets carrying scientific instruments in "artificial satellites," 1,200 miles above sea level.

LINDBERGH'S "SPIRIT OF ST. LOUIS"

AMERICAN AIRLINES   NORTH WEST ORIENT   PAN AMERICAN

THE SYMBOLS below once represented the essentials, or niceties, and a few luxuries of civilized living. The companies are still going strong.

INDIAN HEAD MILLS
COTTON SHEETING—1835

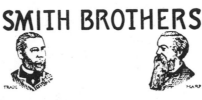

SMITH BROTHERS
COUGH DROPS—1847

AMERICAN THREAD COMPANY
YARNS—1863

SINGER MANUFACTURING CO.
SEWING MACHINES—1865

COLT'S PATENT FIRE ARMS
GUNS—1873

PILLSBURY'S
FLOUR—1870

CRANE AND COMPANY
WRITING PAPERS—1875

QUAKER OATS COMPANY
CEREALS—1878

STEINWAY & SONS
PIANOS—1878

P. BALLANTINE & SONS
BEER—1880

LYDIA E. PINKHAM, COMPANY
MEDICAL PREPARATIONS—1881

EASTMAN KODAK COMPANY
CAMERAS—1888

NIXDORF-KREIN MFG. COMPANY
WAGONS & YOKES—1885

WILBUR-SUCHARD COMPANY
CHOCOLATES & COCOA—1887

BULL DURHAM
TOBACCO—1864

Organizations

INDUSTRIAL, BUSINESS AND PROFESSIONAL ORGANIZATIONS

SINCE THE MEMBERS of the Mayflower Pact may be thought of as the founders of an organization, it is no wonder that Americans formed organizations to cover almost all aspects of their lives. Below are some of the industrial, business, and professional groups which have influenced the American scene, the economy, and democratic values.

AMERICAN MEDICAL ASSOCIATION

CONGRESS OF INDUSTRIAL ORGANIZATIONS

AS EARLY as 1835 the French writer de Tocqueville had commented on the fact that Americans formed committees to solve community problems. Since illness is a community problem, organizations were formed to raise money and carry on research. The lowering of the TB and polio rates are only two of the many benefits of these volunteer groups who have done and are doing so much.

Top Row: The American Cancer Society, The National Tuberculosis Association, The National Society for Crippled Children and Adults, The American Heart Association; **Second Row:** The American Red Cross, The National Association for Mental Health, The Salvation Army; **Third Row:** United Community Funds & Councils of America, The Greater New York Fund, Arthritis & Rheumatism Foundation; **Bottom Row:** United Cerebral Palsy Association, Muscular Dystrophy Associations of America, National Foundation for Infantile Paralysis.

MAN IS A GREGARIOUS animal, and Americans are no exceptions. Indeed, to the rest of the world, Americans are the most gregarious of all humans. As a result we have been called "The Society of Joiners." Organizations exist for hobbyists. There are religious groups and national groups, philanthropic organizations and the social groups. The next two pages present a selection of the social organizations.

Top Row: Odd Fellows, 1819; Rebekah Degree; *Second Row:* Society of the Cincinnati, 1783; Red Men, 1834; Daughters of Pocahontas; Foresters of America, 1832; *Third Row:* Ancient Order of Hibernians, 1836; Knights of Pythias, 1864; Pythian Sisters; B'nai B'rith, 1843; *Bottom Row:* National Grange, 1867; Knights of Columbus, 1882; Daughters of Isabella; Elks, 1868.

Top Row: Royal Neighbors; Orioles; Sons of the American Revolution, 1889; Daughters of the American Revolution, 1890; *Second Row:* Royal Arcanum, 1877; Maccabees, 1878; United Commercial Travelers, 1888; Woodsmen of the World, 1890; *Third Row:* Eagles, 1898; Owls, 1904; Rotary International, 1905; National Exchange Club, 1890; *Bottom Row:* Kiwanis International, 1915; Lions International, 1917; Optimist International, 1919; Knights of Malta.

FREEMASONRY WAS brought to America before 1730. Its aim was and is the moral and spiritual elevation of mankind. The masonic order for boys is the De Molay.

Top Row: Mystic Shrine, Thirty-Third Degree Masons, White Star of Jerusalem, Rose, Croix; *Second Row:* Thirty-Second Degree Masons, Knights Templars, Council of Kadosh, Council of Royal and Select Masters; *Third Row:* Council of the Princes of Jerusalem, Lodge of Perfection, Blue Lodge, Tall Cedars of Lebanon; *Bottom Row:* Grotto, Eastern Star, Rainbow Girls, Royal Arch.

OF ALL the emblems below the most coveted is the Congressional Medal of Honor, established by Congress in 1862, and rendered to those who have risked their lives in battle beyond the call of duty.

Top Row: Army Medal of Honor, the United States Army, the United States Navy, the Navy Medal of Honor; *Second Row:* Marine Corps, Coast Guard, National Guard, Merchant Marine; *Third Row:* Air Corps, Army Air Force, Navy Aviation, Women's Army Corps—WACS; *Bottom Row:* Construction Battalion—Seabees—of the United States Navy; WAVES—Women Accepted for Volunteer Emergency Service—The United States Navy, SPARS—Semper Paratus Always Ready—Women's Corp of The United States Coast Guard, Army Emergency Relief.

THE FIRST VETERANS organization in the United States was the GAR—or Grand Army of the Republic, organized in Springfield, Ill., 1865.

Top Row: American Legion, 1919; American Legion Auxiliary; American Veterans Committee, 1945; *Second Row:* American Veterans of World War II, 1947; Catholic War Veterans, 1935; Disabled American Veterans, 1923; *Third Row:* The Forty and Eight, 1920; Grand Army of the Republic, 1865; Honorable Discharge Button, World War II; *Fourth Row:* Jewish War Veterans, 1896; United Spanish War Veterans, 1904; Veterans of Foreign Wars, 1913; *Bottom Row:* Veterans of Foreign Wars Auxiliary; Women's Army Corps and Veterans Association; Women's Relief Corps, Grand Army Auxiliary.

"AS THE TWIG is bent . . ." Below are a selection of the organizations a youth can join and enjoy in the United States.

Top Row: American Youth Hostels, 1934; Baptist Youth Fellowship, 1941; Boys Club of America, 1906; **Second Row:** Boy Scouts of America, 1910; Camp Fire Girls, 1910; Catholic Youth Organization, 1936; **Third Row:** 4-H Clubs, 1900; Girl Scouts of the U.S.A., 1912; Junior Achievement, 1919; **Fourth Row:** Little League Baseball, 1939; Methodist Youth Fellowship, 1939; Walter League Lutheran Youth, 1893; **Bottom Row:** Young Men's Hebrew Association, 1874; Young Men's Christian Association, 1844; Young Women's Christian Association of the U.S.A., 1858.

Colleges and Universities

ALMOST THREE and one-half million students are enrolled in American colleges and universities, some of which are listed on these pages and pages 52 and 53.

Our National Sport

AMERICAN AND NATIONAL LEAGUE BASEBALL TEAMS

ALTHOUGH BASEBALL was played before 1839, that is its date of origin, and Abner Doubleday, of Cooperstown, N. Y. is its "inventor." The National League was organized in 1876; the American League in 1901. The first curve was thrown by William A. (Candy) Cummings, in 1867. Three-strike rule: 1887. Four-ball pass came in 1889. Pitching distance set at 60½ feet in 1893.

PLAYING BALL

AMERICAN LEAGUE

| NEW YORK YANKEES | MINNESOTA TWINS | WASHINGTON SENATORS | CLEVELAND INDIANS | DETROIT TIGERS |

| CHICAGO WHITE SOX | CALIFORNIA ANGELS | KANSAS CITY ATHLETICS | BALTIMORE ORIOLES | BOSTON RED SOX |

NATIONAL LEAGUE

| SAN FRANCISCO GIANTS | ST. LOUIS CARDINALS | LOS ANGELES DODGERS | ATLANTA BRAVES | NEW YORK METS |

| PITTSBURGH PIRATES | HOUSTON ASTROS | CINCINNATI REDS | PHILADELPHIA PHILLIES | CHICAGO CUBS |

Comic Strips

CLASSICS AND CURRENT

THE FIRST COLORED cartoon appeared in the *New York World*, 1895. It was "The Yellow Kid" by Richard Outcault. In 1907 the first strip of cartoons made history, and made the first characters in it—"Mutt & Jeff" by Bud Fisher—immortal. Since then these "comic strips" have multiplied by the hundreds and are read by more than 100,000,000 people every day. Besides those shown below, old favorites are "The Katzenjammer Kids," "Joe Palooka," "Terry and the Pirates," "Steve Canyon," "The Gumps," "Gasoline Alley," "Moon Mullins," "Barney Google," "Prince Val," "Tarzan."

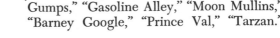

**MUTT & JEFF—BY BUD FISHER
NOW DRAWN BY AL SMITH**

**DICK TRACY
BY CHESTER GOULD**

**KRAZY KAT—BY GEORGE HERRIMAN
THE FIRST SOPHISTICATED STRIP—1911**

**LITTLE ORPHAN ANNIE
BY HAROLD GRAY**

**POGO—AND FRIENDS
BY WALT KELLY**

**L'IL ABNER
BY AL CAPP**

BRINGING UP FATHER—BY GEORGE McMANUS

Democracy in Action

ON THE FOLLOWING four pages are a selection of political symbols which have appeared in American history. Some are well known and were powerful in their day. Others, which wielded little influence, have been forgotten. But all are the result of freedom.

One of the first political cartoons. By Benjamin Franklin, 1774. The parts of the snake represent the thirteen new colonies — the head stands for all the New England colonies.

The Gerrymander (1812) after Governor Elbridge Gerry of Massachusetts, who was accused by the Federalists of redistricting his state in order to assure his election. The Gerrymander is made up of sections of Massachusetts in this original.

"United Now Alive and Free" by John Holt, 1775. Then the slogan reads: ". . . *And Thus Supported Everbless Our Land • Firm on This Basis Liberty Shall Stand Till Time Becomes Eternity.*"

Anti-Federalist campaign poster against the "Hartford convention candidates." The Hartford convention was a secret Federalist meeting in 1814 of New England Federalists who attacked the policies of Madison and the War of 1812 in particular.

Symbol for the Culpepper Minutemen which used Patrick Henry's *"Liberty or Death"* as well as *"Don't Tread on Me."*

Democratic-Republican Party campaign poster for election of 1816, supporting James Monroe against Rufus King, the Federalist candidate. Monroe won.

Emblem of the Sons of Liberty 1776, organized in opposition to the Stamp Act, given their name by a member of parliament, Samuel Adams, one of its chiefs.

Whig Party (forerunner of the Republican Party) poster for the 1840 campaign. The Whig candidates were Harrison and Tyler. Their slogan was "Log Cabin and Hard Cider."

Democratic-Republican Party label, 1790. Forerunner of the Democratic Party today. Seal shows French liberty cap.

Rooster emblem of Democratic Party in the 1844 election. Polk defeated Clay, the Whig.

EVERY TWO YEARS the U. S. elects the whole House of Representatives and one-third of the Senate. Every four years, in the years divisible by four, the President and Vice-President are also elected. From these contests have come the political parties and their emblems, our law-makers, judges, and leaders.

Party symbol for Democratic National Committee—1852, The "Five Pointed Star."

Symbol of the Ku Klux Klan, the invisible empire of the Kuklos, founded at Pulaski, Tennessee, after the Civil War (1866). It declined in the 1870's, after federal legislation; rose again in the 1920's and the 1930's.

Sagenichts campaign emblem against the American (Know Nothing) Party, used in the 1856 presidential race. When asked about the motives, or purpose of their group, members of the American party would say: *"I Know Nothing."* Fillmore was their candidate and he received eight electoral votes, losing to James Buchanan, the Democrat, and John C. Fremont, the Republican candidate.

Seal of the Knights of Labor, organized in 1896, and—up to that time—the most important labor group in the country. Motto reads: *"That Is The Most Perfect Government, In Which An Injury to One Is The Concern Of All."*

Two years after the Democrats formed a national committee, the Republican Party formed their committee, too—1854. They used the eagle symbol.

Democratic party symbol — the donkey—created by the political cartoonist of the day, Thomas Nast—in 1870.

Emblem and slogan of the Confederate States (1861-1865) with their motto: *"No Country, No Fatherland That Does Not Keep Faith."*

Tammany Hall tiger, also by Nast—1871. Tammany Hall is the headquarters of the New York County Democratic Committee, New York City. The name comes from the Delaware Indian language, meaning tribal chief. The first Tammany societies were organized in New York, 1783.

Republican Party campaign symbol for the election of 1864, which chose Abraham Lincoln for his second term. During this campaign the Republican Party was called the Union Party. The Democratic Party of the northern states ran G. B. McClellan, the general whom Lincoln had replaced with Ulysses S. Grant.

LIBERTY
AND
UNION

ONE AND INSEPARABLE

Thomas Nast also first drew the elephant representing the Republican Party—1874. Nast did his work for the magazine *Harper's Weekly.*

Top Row: Greenback Party, founded 1876; Socialist Labor Party of America, 1877; "Grand Old Party"—Republican Campaign Slogan, 1880; Socialist Party, 1899; *Second Row:* Alabama Democratic Campaign Symbol, 1901; Industrial Workers of the World, the "Wobblies," 1904; NAACP, National Association for the Advancement of Colored People, 1909; Bull Moose Party, for Theodore Roosevelt, 1912; *Third Row:* Independent Party, 1912; Democratic Campaign Slogan for Wilson, 1916; League of Women Voters, 1918; Communist Party of the U.S.A., 1919; *Fourth Row:* Prohibition Party Symbol for 1920 Campaign; Camel symbol for Prohibition Party, 1920; Farmer-Labor Party, 1924; Democratic Campaign Symbol for Alfred E. Smith, 1928; *Bottom Row:* Workers Party of America, 1929; Recovery Party, 1933; Proletarian Party, 1936; Progressive Party (La Follette), 1936.

THE FIRST TUESDAY after the first Monday in November was chosen as election day by Congress in 1845. But the American people have never directly elected the President and Vice-President. They have voted for members of the Electoral College. Voters in each state choose a number of Electors equal to the number of Congressmen in that state—535 for the whole country. The Electors then vote for their party's candidates. Since 1828, when Jackson defeated John Quincy Adams, the presidential elections have been primarily between the two major parties: Democratic and Republican. (*See pages 68 and 69 for the Presidents.*)

Top Row: Townsend Plan Party, 1936; Buffalo Symbol of Townsend Plan Party, 1936; New Deal, 1936; American Labor Party, founded 1937; *Second Row:* Trades Union, 1937; Socialist Workers Party, founded 1938; Republican Campaign slogan for Wendell L. Wilkie, 1940; CIO-Political Action Committee; *Third Row:* Democratic Campaign Emblem for Franklin D. Roosevelt, 1944; Liberal Party of New York, founded 1944; People's Rights Party, 1946; Americans for Democratic Action, 1947; *Bottom Row:* AFL—Labor League for Political Education, founded 1947; Progressive Party for Henry Wallace, 1948; Freedom and Union, 1950; Republican Campaign Symbol for Dwight D. Eisenhower, 1952.

The Federal Government

EXECUTIVE, LEGISLATIVE, AND JUDICIAL

The counterfeiting laws of the United States prohibit the reproduction of "anything in the likeness of the currency of the U.S. or any part thereof." Since the Seal of the Treasury is on currency, it cannot be shown.

THE USE OF historic symbols is often joined to modern posters when the U. S. government wants to speak to the people, particularly in time of war. Below can be seen the eagle, Minuteman, stars of the thirteen colonies, and Uncle Sam's profile. One page 66 can be seen Uncle Sam again, and the Statue of Liberty.

Top Row: National Recovery Administration, 1933, ruled unconstitutional by Supreme Court in 1935; Tennessee Valley Authority, 1933; *Second Row:* Works Projects Administration, 1935, the WPA; Army Air Corps Recruiting poster, 1941; Women's Voluntary Services, 1942; *Third Row:* National Victory Garden Institute, 1942; Maritime Commission, 1942; War Food Administration, 1942; *Fourth Row:* Office of Defense Transportation, 1942; War Production Board, 1942; Office of Defense Administration, 1942; *Bottom Row:* Victory Book Campaign, 1942; Health and Welfare Services, 1942; First War Loan, 1942.

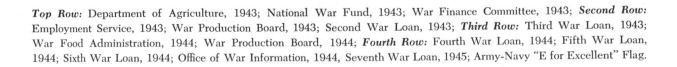

Top Row: Department of Agriculture, 1943; National War Fund, 1943; War Finance Committee, 1943; **Second Row:** Employment Service, 1943; War Production Board, 1943; Second War Loan, 1943; **Third Row:** Third War Loan, 1943; War Food Administration, 1944; War Production Board, 1944; **Fourth Row:** Fourth War Loan, 1944; Fifth War Loan, 1944; Sixth War Loan, 1944; Office of War Information, 1944, Seventh War Loan, 1945; Army-Navy "E for Excellent" Flag.

Top Row: Victory Loan, 1945; War Assets Administration, 1946; War Assets Administration, 1946; *Second Row:* Veterans Organizations, 1946; Army Air Force, 1947 (Air Force became separate branch of National Military Establishment July 26, 1947); Office of Price Stabilization, 1951; *Third Row:* Economic Co-operation Administration, 1951; Army Air Force Recruiting Service, 1951; Security Loan, 1951; *Fourth Row:* Forest Service, Department of Agriculture; Forest Service, Department of Agriculture; Nuclear Radiation warning poster, Atomic Energy Commission; *Bottom Row:* Civilian Defense, Air Raid Public Shelter Sign; Civil Air Patrol.

Elected Leaders

THE PRESIDENTS

ARTICLE II OF THE CONSTITUTION states that "The executive Power shall be vested in a President of the United States of America. . . ." The only qualifications are that he be "a natural born Citizen, or a Citizen of the United States," that he "have attained to the age of thirty five Years, and been fourteen years a Resident within the United States." Below are those who were elected to that office since 1788. There are thirty-five of them. Soldiers, lawyers, a college president. Rich men, and not so rich. Our great leaders—who led us to greatness in less than 200 years.

GEORGE WASHINGTON
(1732-99) 1789-97

JOHN ADAMS *(1735-1826)*
2nd President, 1797-1801

THOMAS JEFFERSON
(1743-1826) 1801-09

JAMES MADISON
(1751-1836) 1809-17

JAMES MONROE *(1758-1831)*
5th President, 1817-25

JOHN QUINCY ADAMS
(1767-1848) 1825-29

ANDREW JACKSON
(1767-1845) 1829-37

MARTIN VAN BUREN
(1782-1862) 1837-41

WILLIAM H. HARRISON
(1773-1841) 1841

JOHN TYLER *(1790-1862)*
10th President, 1841-45

JAMES KNOX POLK
(1795-1849) 1845-49

ZACHARY TAYLOR
(1784-1850) 1849-50

MILLARD FILLMORE
(1800-74) 1850-53

FRANKLIN PIERCE *(1804-69)*
14th President *(1853-57)*

JAMES BUCHANAN
(1791-1868) 1857-61

ABRAHAM LINCOLN *(1809-65)*
16th President *(1861-65)*

ANDREW JOHNSON
(1808-1875) 1865-69

ULYSSES S. GRANT
(1822-1885) 1869-77

RUTHERFORD B. HAYES
(1822-1893) 1877-81

JAMES A. GARFIELD
(1831-81) 1881

CHESTER A. ARTHUR
(1830-86) 1881-85

GROVER CLEVELAND
(1837-1908) 1885-89, '93-'97

BENJAMIN HARRISON
(1833-1901) 1889-93

WILLIAM McKINLEY
(1843-1901) 1897-1901

THEODORE ROOSEVELT
(1858-1919) 1901-09

WILLIAM H. TAFT
(1857-1930) 1909-13

WOODROW WILSON
(1856-1924) 1913-21

WARREN C. HARDING
(1865-1923) 1921-23

CALVIN COOLIDGE
(1872-1933) 1923-29

HERBERT HOOVER
(1874-1964) 1929-33

FRANKLIN D. ROOSEVELT
(1882-1945) 1933-45

HARRY S. TRUMAN
(1884-) 1945-53

DWIGHT D. EISENHOWER
(1890-) 1953-61

JOHN F. KENNEDY
(1917-1963) 1961-63

LYNDON B. JOHNSON
(1908-) 1963-

ALTHOUGH THERE ARE only 35 illustrations on these two pages, there have been 36 Presidents: Grover Cleveland served twice. He was 22nd President from 1885 to 1889. Benjamin Harrison was 23rd from 1889 to 1893, and Cleveland was 24th from 1893 to 1897. Eight Vice-Presidents have assumed the office upon the death of the President: Tyler, Fillmore, Andrew Johnson, Arthur, Theodore Roosevelt, Coolidge, Truman and Lyndon Johnson. Of these, the last four were subsequently reelected.

The Fifty States: A GAZETTE

ALABAMA

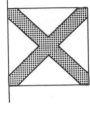
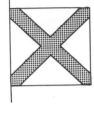

Capital: Montgomery.
Largest City: Birmingham.
Nicknames: Cotton State; Yellowhammer State.
Motto: "We dare defend our rights."
Song: "Alabama."
Abbreviation: Ala.
Tree: Southern Pine.
Flower: Goldenrod.
Bird: Yellowhammer.
22nd State to enter Union, Dec. 14, 1819.
*28th in area: 51,609 square miles

ALASKA

Capital: Juneau.
Largest City: Anchorage.
Song: "Alaska's Flag."
Abbreviation: Spelled out.
Tree: Sitka Spruce.
Bird: Willow Ptarmigan.
Flower: Forget-Me-Not.
49th State to enter Union, January 3, 1959.
First in area: 586,400 sq. mi. (including Aleutian Islands).

Except in the Alaska and Hawaii entries, this figure gives the size order of the states prior to the admission of Alaska and Hawaii.

ARIZONA

Capital: Phoenix.
Largest City: Phoenix.
Nicknames: Grand
  Canyon State; Sunset
  State; Apache State.
Motto: "God Enriches."
Song: "Arizona."
Abbreviation: Ariz.
Tree: None.
Flower: Saguaro Cactus.
Bird: Cactus Wren.
  48th State to enter
Union, Feb. 14, 1912. 5th
in area: 113,909 sq. mi.

NO STATE TREE

Phoenix ★

ARIZONA

ARKANSAS

Capital: Little Rock.
Largest City: Little Rock.
Nicknames: Land of
  Opportunity; Wonder
  State; Bear State.
Motto: "The People Rule."
Song: "The Arkansas
  Traveler."
Abbreviation: Ark.
Tree: Pine.
Flower: Apple Blossom.
Bird: Mockingbird.
  25th State to enter
Union, June 15, 1836. 26th
in area: 53,102 sq. mi.

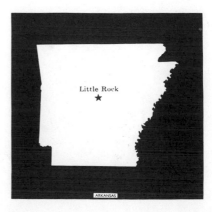

Little Rock ★

ARKANSAS

CALIFORNIA

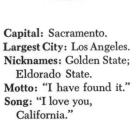

Capital: Sacramento.
Largest City: Los Angeles.
Nicknames: Golden State;
Eldorado State.
Motto: "I have found it."
Song: "I love you,
California."
Abbreviation: Cal.
Tree: Redwood
(Sequoia).
Flower: Golden Poppy.
Bird: California Valley
Quail.
  31st State to enter
Union, Sept. 9, 1850. 2nd
in area: 158,693 sq. mi.

COLORADO

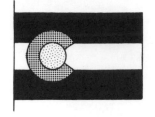

Capital: Denver.
Largest City: Denver.
Nickname: Centennial
State.
Motto: 'Nothing without
Providence"
Song: "Where the
Colombines Grow."
Abbreviation: Colo.
Tree: Blue Spruce.
Flower: Rocky Mountain
Columbine.
Bird: Lark Bunting.
  38th State to enter
Union, Aug. 1, 1876. 7th
in area: 104,247 sq. mi.

CONNECTICUT

Capital: Hartford.
Largest City: Hartford.
Nicknames: Constitution
State; Nutmeg State.
Motto: "He who trans-
planted continues to
sustain."
Song: None.
Abbreviation: Conn.
Tree: White Oak.
Flower: Mountain Laurel.
Bird: Robin.
5th State to enter
Union, Jan 9, 1788. 46th
in area: 5,009 sq. mi.

DELAWARE

Capital: Dover.
Largest City: Wilmington.
Nicknames: Diamond
State; First State; Hen
State.
Motto: "Liberty and
Independence."
Song: "Our Delaware."
Abbreviation: Del.
Tree: American Holly.
Flower: Peach Blossom.
Bird: Blue Hen Chicken.
1st State to enter
Union, Dec. 7, 1787. 47th
in area: 2,057 sq. mi.

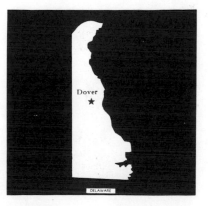

FLORIDA

 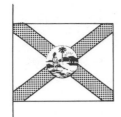

Capital: Tallahassee.
Largest City: Miami.
Nicknames: Peninsula
State; Land of Flowers;
Everglade State.
Motto: "In God We
Trust."
Song: "Swanee River."
Abbreviation: Fla.
Tree: Sabal Palmetto.
Flower: Orange Blossom.
Bird: Mockingbird.
27th State to enter
Union, Mar. 3, 1845. 21st
in area: 58,666 sq. mi.

GEORGIA

Capital: Atlanta.
Largest City: Atlanta.
Nicknames: Cracker
State; Empire State of
the South.
Motto: "Wisdom, Justice,
and Moderation."
Song: "Georgia."
Abbreviation: Ga.
Tree: Live Oak.
Flower: Cherokee Rose.
Bird: Brown Thrasher.
4th State to enter
Union, Jan. 2, 1788. 20th
in area: 58,876 sq. mi.

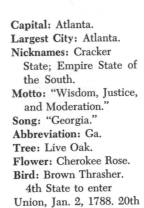 

HAWAII

Capital: Honolulu.
Islands: Hawaii, Maui, Kahoolawe, Lanai, Molokai, Oahu, Kavai, Nihau.
Largest City: Honolulu.
Nickname: The Aloha State.
Motto: "The Life of the Land is Preserved by Righteousness."
Song: "Hawaii Ponoi."
Tree: Kukul.
Bird: Nene.
Flower: Hibiscus.
50th State to enter Union, August 21, 1959. 47th in area: 6,454 sq. mi.

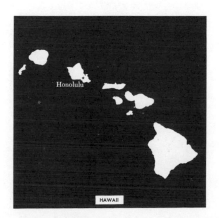

IDAHO

Capital: Boise.
Largest City: Boise.
Nicknames: Gem State; Gem of the Mountains.
Motto: "Mayest Thou Endure Forever."
Song: "Here We Have Idaho."
Abbreviation: Spelled out.
Tree: Western White Pine.
Flower: Syringa.
Bird: Mountain Bluebird.
43rd State to enter Union, July 3, 1890. 12th in area: 83,557 sq. mi.

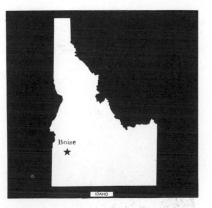

ILLINOIS

Capital: Springfield.
Largest City: Chicago.
Nicknames: Prairie State;
  Sucker State.
Motto: "State Sovereignty
  —National Union."
Song: "Illinois."
Abbreviation: Ill.
Tree: Native Oak.
Flower: Native Violet.
Bird: Cardinal.
  21st State to enter
Union, Dec. 3, 1818. 23rd
in area: 56,400 sq. mi.

INDIANA

Capital: Indianapolis.
Largest City: Indian-
  apolis.
Nickname: Hoosier State.
Motto: "The Crossroads
  of America."
Song: "On the Banks of
  the Wabash, Far
  Away."
Abbreviation: Ind.
Tree: Yellow Poplar.
  (Tulip Tree.)
Flower: Zinnia.
Bird: Cardinal.
  19th State to enter
Union, Dec. 11, 1816. 37th
in area: 36,291 sq. mi.

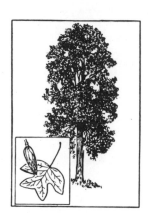

IOWA

 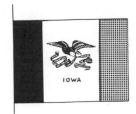

Capital: Des Moines.
Largest City: Des Moines.
Nickname: Hawkeye State.
Motto: "Our Liberties We Prize and Our Rights We Will Maintain."
Song: "Song of Iowa."
Abbreviation: Spelled out.
Tree: None.
Flower: Wild Rose.
Bird: Eastern Goldfinch.
  29th State to enter Union, Dec. 28, 1846. 24th in area: 56,280 sq. mi.

NO STATE TREE

KANSAS

Capital: Topeka.
Largest City: Wichita.
Nicknames: Sunflower State; Jayhawk State.
Motto: "To the Stars Through Difficulties."
Song: "Home on the Range."
Abbreviation: Kans.
Tree: Cottonwood.
Flower: Sunflower.
Bird: Western Meadowlark.
  34th State to enter Union, Jan. 29, 1861. 13th in area: 82,276 sq. mi.

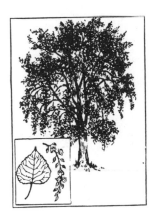

KENTUCKY

Capital: Frankfort.
Largest City: Louisville.
Nickname: Blue Grass
State.
Motto: "United We Stand,
Divided We Fall."
Song: "My Old Kentucky
Home."
Abbreviation: Ky.
Tree: Yellow Poplar
(Tulip Tree).
Flower: Goldenrod.
Bird: Kentucky Cardinal.
15th State to enter
Union, June 1, 1792. 36th
in area: 40,395 sq. mi.

LOUISIANA

Capital: Baton Rouge.
Largest City: New
Orleans.
Nicknames: Pelican State;
Creole State.
Motto: "Union, Justice,
and Confidence."
Song: "Song of
Louisiana."
Abbreviation: La.
Tree: None.
Flower: Magnolia.
Bird: Eastern Brown
Pelican.
18th State to enter
Union, April 30, 1812.
30th in area: 48,523
sq. mi.

NO
STATE
TREE

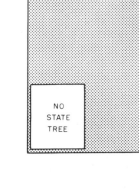

MAINE

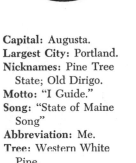

Capital: Augusta.
Largest City: Portland.
Nicknames: Pine Tree State; Old Dirigo.
Motto: "I Guide."
Song: "State of Maine Song"
Abbreviation: Me.
Tree: Western White Pine.
Flower: White Pine Cone & Tassel.
Bird: Chickadee.
23rd State to enter Union, March 15, 1820.
38th in area: 33,215 sq. mi.

MARYLAND

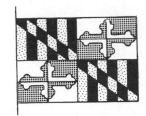 

Capital: Annapolis.
Largest City: Baltimore.
Nicknames: Free State: Old Line State.
Motto: "Manly deeds, Womanly Words."
Song: "Maryland! My Maryland!"
Abbreviation: Md.
Tree: White Oak.
Flower: Black-eyed Susan.
Bird: Baltimore Oriole.
7th State to enter Union, April 28, 1788.
41st in area: 10,577 sq. mi.

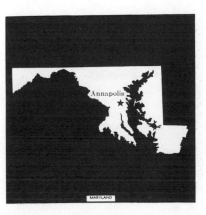

MASSACHUSETTS

MICHIGAN

Capital: Boston.
Largest City: Boston.
Nicknames: Bay State;
   Old Colony State.
Motto: "By the Sword
   We Seek Peace, But
   Peace only Under
   Liberty."
Song: "Massachusetts."
Abbreviation: Mass.
Tree: American Elm.
Flower: Mayflower.
Bird: Chickadee.
   6th State to enter
Union, Feb. 6, 1788. 44th
in area: 8,257 sq. mi.

Capital: Lansing.
Largest City: Detroit.
Nickname: Wolverine
   State.
Motto: "If You Seek a
   Pleasant Peninsula,
   Look About You."
Song: "Michigan, My
   Michigan."
Abbreviation: Mich.
Tree: Apple.
Flower: Apple Blossom.
Bird: Robin.
   26th State to enter
Union, Jan. 26, 1827. 22nd
in area: 58,216 sq. mi.

MINNESOTA

Capital: St. Paul.
Largest City: Minne-
apolis.
Nicknames: North Star
State; Gopher State.
Motto: "The Star of the
North."
Song: "Hail Minnesota!"
Abbreviation: Minn.
Tree: Eastern White Pine.
Flower: Moccasin Flower.
Bird: American Goldfinch.
32nd State to enter
Union, May 11, 1858. 11th
in area: 84,068 sq. mi.

MISSISSIPPI

Capital: Jackson.
Largest City: Jackson
Nicknames: Magnolia
State; Bayou State.
Motto: "By Valor and
Arms."
Song: "Way Down South
in Mississippi."
Abbreviation: Miss.
Tree: Southern Magnolia.
Flower: Magnolia.
Bird: Mockingbird.
20th State to enter
Union, Dec. 10, 1817. 31st
in area: 47,716 sq. mi.

MISSOURI

Capital: Jefferson City.
Largest City: St. Louis.
Nicknames: Show-Me State; Ozark State.
Motto: "Let the Welfare of the People Be the Supreme Law."
Song: "Missouri Waltz."
Abbreviation: Mo.
Tree: None.
Flower: Hawthorn.
Bird: Bluebird.
  24th State to enter Union, Aug. 10, 1821. 18th in area: 69,674 sq. mi.

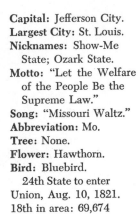

NO STATE TREE

MONTANA

Capital: Helena.
Largest City: Great Falls.
Nicknames: Treasure State; Bonanza State.
Motto: "Gold and Silver."
Song: "Montana."
Abbreviation: Mont.
Tree: Ponderosa Pine.
Flower: Bitterroot.
Bird: Western Meadow-lark.
  41st State to enter Union, Nov. 8, 1889. 3rd in area: 147,138 sq. mi.

NEBRASKA

NEVADA

Capital: Lincoln.
Largest City: Omaha.
Nicknames: Cornhusker
State; Antelope State.
Motto: Equality Before
the Law.
Song: "My Nebraska"
(unofficial).
Abbreviation: Neb.
Tree: American Elm.
Flower: Goldenrod.
Bird: Western Meadow-
lark.
    37th State to enter
Union, Mar. 1, 1867. 14th
in area: 77,237 sq. mi.

Capital: Carson City.
Largest City: Reno.
Nicknames: Silver State;
Sagebrush State.
Motto: "All For Our
Country."
Song: "Home Means
Nevada."
Abbreviation: Nev.
Tree: Trembling Aspen.
Flower: Sagebrush.
Bird: Mountain Bluebird.
    36th State to enter
Union, Oct. 31, 1864. 6th
in area: 110,540 sq. mi.

NEW HAMPSHIRE

NEW JERSEY

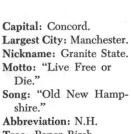

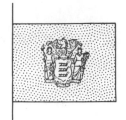

Capital: Concord.
Largest City: Manchester.
Nickname: Granite State.
Motto: "Live Free or Die."
Song: "Old New Hampshire."
Abbreviation: N.H.
Tree: Paper Birch.
Flower: Purple Lilac.
Bird: Purple Finch.
9th State to enter Union, June 21, 1788. 43rd in area: 9,304 sq. mi.

Capital: Trenton.
Largest City: Newark.
Nickname: Garden State.
Motto: "Liberty and Prosperity."
Song: New Jersey Loyalty Song.
Abbreviation: N.J.
Tree: Northern Red Oak.
Flower: Violet.
Bird: Eastern Goldfinch.
3rd State to enter Union, Dec. 18, 1787. 45th in area: 7,836 sq. mi.

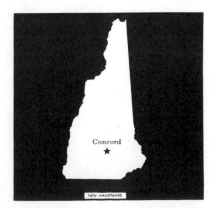

NEW MEXICO

Capital: Sante Fe.
Largest City: Albuquerque.
Nicknames: Land of Enchantment; Cactus State; Sunshine State.
Motto: "We Grow As We Go."
Song: "O, Fair New Mexico."
Abbreviation: N.M.
Tree: Pinyon.
Flower: Yucca.
Bird: Road Runner.
47th State to enter Union, Jan. 6, 1912. 4th in area: 121,666 sq. mi.

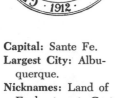

NEW YORK

Capital: Albany.
Largest City: New York.
Nicknames: Empire State; Excelsior State.
Motto: Excelsior ("Ever Upward.")
Song: None.
Abbreviation: N.Y.
Tree: Sugar Maple.
Flower: Rose.
Bird: Bluebird.
11th State to enter Union, July 26, 1788. 29th in area: 49,576 sq. mi.

NORTH CAROLINA

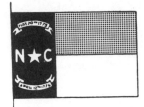

Capital: Raleigh.
Largest City: Charlotte.
Nickname: Tar Heel
State.
Motto: "To Be Rather
Than To Seem."
Song: "The Old North
State."
Abbreviation: N.C.
Tree: None.
Flower: Dogwood.
Bird: Cardinal.
12th State to enter
Union, Nov. 21, 1789.
27th in area: 52,712
sq. mi.

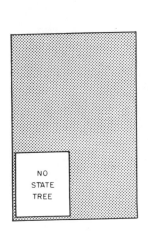

NO STATE TREE

NORTH CAROLINA

NORTH DAKOTA

Capital: Bismarck.
Largest City: Fargo.
Nicknames: Flickertail
State; Sioux State.
Motto: "Liberty and
Union, Now and For-
ever, One and
Inseparable."
Song: "North Dakota
Hymn."
Abbreviation: N.D.
Tree: American Elm.
Flower: Wild Prairie
Rose.
Bird: Western Meadow-
lark.
39th State to enter
Union, Nov. 2, 1889. 16th
in area: 70,665 sq. mi.

Bismarck

NORTH DAKOTA

OHIO

 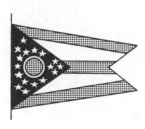

Capital: Columbus.
Largest City: Cleveland.
Nickname: Buckeye State.
Motto: None.
Song: None officially.
Abbreviation: Spelled out.
Tree: Buckeye.
Flower: Scarlet
  Carnation.
Bird: Cardinal.
  17th State to enter
Union, March 1, 1803.
34th in area: 41,222
sq. mi.

OKLAHOMA

Capital: Oklahoma City.
Largest City: Oklahoma
  City.
Nickname: Sooner State.
Motto: "Labor Conquers
  All Things."
Song: "Oklahoma."
Abbreviation: Okla.
Tree: Eastern Redbud.
Flower: Mistletoe.
Bird: Scissor-tailed Fly-
  catcher.
  46th State to enter
Union, Nov. 16, 1907.
17th in area: 69,919
sq. mi.

OREGON

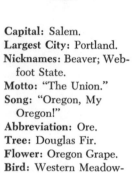

Capital: Salem.
Largest City: Portland.
Nicknames: Beaver; Web-foot State.
Motto: "The Union."
Song: "Oregon, My Oregon!"
Abbreviation: Ore.
Tree: Douglas Fir.
Flower: Oregon Grape.
Bird: Western Meadow-lark.
  33rd State to enter Union, Feb. 14, 1859. 9th in area: 96,981 sq. mi.

PENNSYLVANIA

Capital: Harrisburg.
Largest City: Philadel-phia.
Nicknames: Keystone State; Coal State.
Motto: "Virtue, Liberty and Independence."
Song: None, officially.
Abbreviation: Pa.
Tree: Eastern Hemlock.
Flower: Mountain Laurel.
Bird: Ruffed Grouse.
  2nd State to enter Union, Dec. 12, 1787. 32nd in area: 45,333 sq. mi.

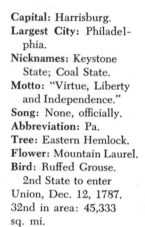

RHODE ISLAND

Capital: Providence.
Largest City. Providence.
Nicknames: Little Rhody;
  Plantation State.
Motto: "Hope."
Song: "Rhode Island."
Abbreviation: R. I.
Tree: Maple.
Flower: Violet.
Bird: Bobwhite.
  13th State to enter
Union, May 29, 1790.
48th in area: 1,214 sq. mi.

SOUTH CAROLINA

Capital: Columbia.
Largest City: Columbia.
Nickname: Palmetto
  State.
Motto: "Prepared in
  Minds and Resources."
Song: "Carolina."
Abbreviation: S. C.
Tree: Cabbage Palmetto.
Flower: Carolina Yellow
  Jessamine.
Bird: Carolina Wren.
  8th State to enter
Union, May 23, 1788.
39th in area: 31,055
sq. mi.

SOUTH DAKOTA

TENNESSEE

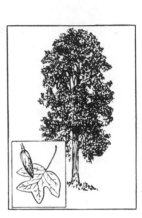

Capital: Pierre.
Largest City: Sioux Falls.
Nicknames: Coyote State, Sunshine State.
Motto: "Under God the People Rule."
Song: "Hail! South Dakota."
Abbreviation: S. D.
Tree: Western White Spruce.
Flower: American Pasqueflower.
Bird: Ring-necked Pheasant.
40th State to enter Union, Nov. 2, 1889. 15th in area: 77,047 sq. mi.

Capital: Nashville.
Largest City: Memphis.
Nicknames: Volunteer State; Big Bend State.
Motto: "Agriculture, Commerce."
Song: "My Homeland, Tennessee."
Abbreviation: Tenn.
Tree: Yellow Poplar (Tulip Tree).
Flower: Iris.
Bird: Mockingbird.
16th State to enter Union, June 1, 1796. 33rd in area: 42,246 sq. mi.

TEXAS

Capital: Austin.
Largest City: Houston.
Nickname: Lone Star State.
Motto: "Friendship."
Song: "Texas, Our Texas."
Abbreviation: Tex.
Tree: Pecan.
Flower: Bluebonnet.
Bird: Mockingbird.
  28th State to enter Union, Dec. 29, 1845. 1st in area: 267,339 sq. mi.

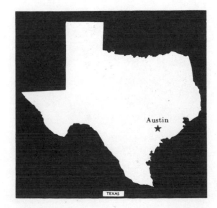

UTAH

Capital: Salt Lake City.
Largest City: Salt Lake City.
Nickname: Beehive State.
Motto: "Industry."
Song: "Utah, We Love Thee."
Abbreviation: Spelled out.
Tree: Blue Spruce.
Flower: Sego Lily.
Bird: Seagull.
  45th State to enter Union, Jan. 4, 1896. 10th in area: 84,916 sq. mi.

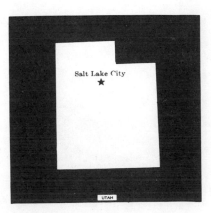

VERMONT

Capital: Montpelier.
Largest City: Burlington.
Nickname: Green Moun-
tain State.
Motto: "Freedom and
Unity."
Song: "Hail to Vermont."
Abbreviation: Vt.
Tree: Sugar Maple.
Flower: Red Clover.
Bird: Hermit Thrush.
14th State to enter
Union, March 4, 1791.
42nd in area: 9,609 sq. mi.

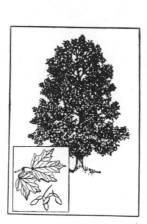

VIRGINIA

Capital: Richmond.
Largest City: Richmond.
Nicknames: Old
Dominion State; Mother
of Presidents.
Motto: 'Thus Ever To
Tyrants.'
Song: "Carry Me Back to
Old Virginny."
Abbreviation: Va.
Tree: Flowering Dog-
wood.
Flower: Dogwood.
Bird: Cardinal.
10th State to enter
Union, June 25, 1788.
35th in area: 40,815
sq. mi.

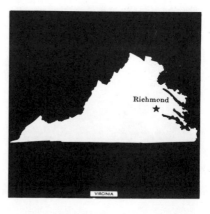

WASHINGTON

Capital: Olympia.
Largest City: Seattle.
Nicknames: Evergreen
　State; Chinook State.
Motto: "Bye and Bye."
Song: "Washington's
　Song."
Abbreviation: Wash.
Tree: Western Hemlock.
Flower: Western
　Rhododendron.
Bird: Willow Goldfinch.
　42nd State to enter
Union, Nov. 11, 1889.
19th in area: 68,192
sq. mi.

WEST VIRGINIA

Capital: Charleston.
Largest City: Huntington.
Nicknames: Panhandle
　State; Mountain State.
Motto: "Mountaineers
　Always Free."
Song: "West Virginia, My
　Home Sweet Home"
　(official); "West
　Virginia Hills"
　(unofficial).
Abbreviation: W. Va.
Tree: Sugar Maple.
Flower: Rhododendron.
Bird: Cardinal.
　35th State to enter
Union, June 20, 1863. 40th
in area: 24,181 sq mi.

WISCONSIN

Capital: Madison.
Largest City: Milwaukee.
Nicknames: Badger State;
  Copper State.
Motto: "Forward."
Song: None officially; "On
  Wisconsin!"
  (unofficially).
Abbreviation: Wis.
Tree: Sugar Maple.
Flower: Violet.
Bird: Robin.
  30th State to enter
Union, May 29, 1848. 25th
in area: 56,154 sq. mi.

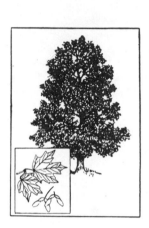

WYOMING

Capital: Cheyenne.
Largest City: Cheyenne.
Nickname: Equality State.
Motto: "Let Arms Yield
  To the Gown."
Song: "Wyoming State
  Song."
Abbreviation: Wyo.
Tree: Cottonwood.
Flower: Indian
  Paintbrush.
Bird: Meadowlark.
  44th State to enter
Union, July 10, 1890.
8th in area: 87,914 sq. mi.